Invisible

A Memoir of the
Rev. William B. Oliver III

CHARLES E. SOULE

Copyright © 2015 Charles E. Soule
All rights reserved.

ISBN: 1502915871
ISBN 13: 9781502915870
Library of Congress Control Number: 2014918904
CreateSpace Independent Publishing Platform
North Charleston, South Carolina

Dedication

This memoir of Bill Oliver is dedicated to all those, past and present, who have had the courage to risk their reputations, their careers, their fortunes, and often their lives in support of social justice, self determination and the marginalized in our society.

Rev. William (Bill) Oliver III

Foreword

This memoir of the Reverend William (Bill) B. Oliver III traces the experiences of a young pastor in East Texas and how he became an activist for civil rights and social justice. The title of this memoir, *Invisible*, came from a phrase used by Bill Oliver in one of my first interviews with him and was repeated frequently as he described the environment in which he had grown up. He said, "blacks were invisible" in the East Texas towns of the 1950s. This phrase will remind many readers of the book *Invisible Man* by Ralph Ellison, published in 1952, which described the circumstances of African Americans in the South at that time.

Many Americans considered the state of Texas to be somewhat separate from the Deep South as far as the extent of segregation and racial prejudice; however, in most ways, East Texas exhibited as much racial discrimination as the states of Alabama, Mississippi, and Louisiana. The Ku Klux Klan was active in this area, and the day-to-day

Jim Crow environment, where blacks were discriminated against in schools, restaurants, hotels, buses, and public facilities and forums, was as ingrained in East Texas society as in the states to the east. An interesting historical fact is that the Texas legislature voted to secede from the Union during the Civil War, opting against secession by only two votes, and a disgusted Governor Sam Houston left the state.

As a young, white, male native of East Texas, brought up in the 1940s and 1950s in a strictly segregated society where blacks were invisible, Bill was an unlikely candidate to assume a leading activist role through demonstrations, sit-ins, and marches in the community of Beaumont, Texas, and beyond. There were many Caucasian ministers from north of the Mason-Dixon Line who participated in civil rights demonstrations, but Bill was unique as a southern boy who became a regionally visible activist in the 1960s and 1970s. It was because of his southern roots that his activities gained him recognition in the press.

As an activist, Bill Oliver was jailed numerous times for participating in nonviolent protests, sit-ins, and marches. On one occasion, he was dragged through the streets of Huntsville, Texas, by the Texas Rangers, causing him to fear for his life. He joined Dr. Martin Luther King Jr. in the 1965 Selma-to-Montgomery march in support of voting rights. Throughout his entire twenty-three years as the pastor of the Plymouth Congregational

Church in Beaumont, he was an activist in numerous civil rights causes and other issues of social justice. Bill's life demonstrates a commitment to helping the marginalized and disenfranchised in our society. Along the way, he became technically proficient in computer systems, which led to a second career later in life.

Bill is a self-effacing individual, not at all prone to talking about his experiences during one of the most tumultuous periods of social upheaval in the twentieth century. When asked how he came to be so involved as an activist, given the segregated environment in which he was raised, his answer was simply, "It was my sense of justice."

I have known Bill Oliver for the past fifteen years, and during that time I gradually became more and more aware of his commitment and activities in support of social justice. In recent years, I suggested to him on several occasions that he should write a book about his personal experiences, for his family and friends if for no one else.

In 2013, over a lunch, I offered to author his memoir and document his unique and fascinating experiences. During the following fifteen months, I met with Bill almost every week, for a total of more than seventy-five hours, listening to him describe in detail his life's history and questioning and urging him to dig deep into his memory. On more than one occasion, his emotions came to the surface, especially when describing incidents involving his parishioners and friends. Frequently his deep spiritual beliefs, especially in the areas of social justice, underscored his determination to be an agent of change.

During my journey with Bill, I have come to appreciate the risks and personal commitment of those who were engaged in the civil rights causes of the '50s, '60s and '70s and to a considerable extent continuing even today. Although Bill Oliver and I are close in age, I was born and educated in an environment where African Americans were "invisible" because they were in fact very few in numbers. I followed the civil rights events of that time with a detached interest from my home in New England, where my wife and I were raising a family of four.

My hope is that readers of this memoir will come to feel and appreciate the experiences of an individual who was not a national leader in civil rights, but a southern boy and a young pastor who came to understand the moral and ethical national problem of the marginalized in our society.

— C. E. Soule

One

EARLY YEARS THROUGH HIGH SCHOOL

Bill Oliver was born on September 5, 1937, in the Methodist church parsonage in the East Texas town of Corrigan. His mother would tell him later that the parsonage window was open, and she listened to the church music between labor pains. She said, "I thought the church service would never end." His mother was a schoolteacher, and three years later she also gave birth to a daughter, Charlotte.

His father, William B. Oliver Jr., was the pastor of the local Methodist church, and while Bill was growing up, his father held several Methodist pastorates throughout East Texas. His father was also a preacher's kid, the

Invisible

son of William B. Oliver, Bill's grandfather, who was a pastor of numerous Disciples of Christ churches in Kentucky, Illinois, and Texas. Bill's father was brought up in the Disciples of Christ tradition but left it as a young adult because he felt the theology was too literal and fundamentalist.

Protestant ministers expected that they would move from one church to another every few years, depending upon the wishes of the church hierarchy or the wishes of their congregations. In the Methodist church, the bishop maintained control of where and when a pastor moved. Bill says his family lived somewhat in fear of the Methodist bishop's annual reading of the appointments list. During Bill's public school years, his father served pastorates in the Texas towns of Corrigan, Fairfield, Daisetta, New London, Texarkana, and Winnie. Bill remembers the moves well—the frequent and sometimes difficult adjustment to new surroundings and the constant making of new friends. He especially remembers the chore of packing and carrying his father's large collection of books from one location to another. For most ministers, their libraries were as essential as their shoes.

Ministers, then as now, were often not well compensated, and Bill remembers on occasion coming home and finding the kitchen table full of canned vegetables and fruit, along with root vegetables. This was the congregation's attempt to supplement his father's salary, and the events were called *poundings*. During the rationing years of World War II, the congregation would often pass on unused ration stamps, even though they would have to go without desired products like sugar and meat. Ration stamps for gasoline were especially important, since they allowed the minister to make rounds visiting his parishioners, and in Bill's father's churches, the parishioners were often scattered across the countryside.

Bill's sister, Charlotte, was born on his third birthday. He had the normal reactions of a first child to the birth of a sibling, someone who would compete for his parents' attention. On that day, an upset child described his birthday cake with coconut frosting as having "little white worms all over it." Not long afterward, he told his parents, "You picked this one, and I want to send her back."

As a minister's son, he was more visible than most children in the community, but that did not deter him from the usual pranks and stunts with which young boys tend to become involved. He rang the church bell in the middle of communion at age four, and on one occasion, he disturbed the Sunday service by taking his younger sister's baby bottle. He risked serious injury climbing oil rigs with friends for sport, in defiance of his parents' wishes. On another occasion, he and a friend were out camping and accidentally started a fire that got so out of control it required the fire department to extinguish. To this day, he's sure no one knows who the culprits were. He recalls, as a sixth grader, smoking cigarettes surreptitiously until being caught by his mother. She turned the discipline over to Bill's father, who told him that he didn't want him to smoke behind his back. "If you're going to smoke, then I want you to do it in the open. Carry them out it the open, in your shirt pocket, like others do." That seemed to cure Bill's youthful defiance, and the only smoking he did after that was a pipe when he was in divinity school.

He recalls being given an anatomy book by his father when he thought Bill was old enough to learn about the birds and the bees. The descriptive pictures in the book were enlightening to Bill, and he shared them with a neighbor friend. His friend told his own father, whereupon Bill's father received significant criticism.

He remembers the thrill of shooting his first deer, a six-point buck, when he was eleven, part of the passage to adulthood for a young man in Texas. One of the benefits of being the minister's son was that he received free admission to the local movie theater, a perk he took advantage of frequently.

Bill emphasizes that "East Texas was the South. Blacks were invisible." There were no blacks in any of the public schools he went to and none in the three colleges he later attended. Not until he attended seminary at Southern Methodist University (SMU) did he encounter blacks in the classroom, and even then, only a token number. That was the environment in the South in the 40s, '50s, and early '60s. Although blacks were a large part of in the population, they were not only segregated physically, but the white population was essentially ignorant of their plight. They were excluded from most public facilities, they shopped in stores that catered to blacks, and they were excluded from most recreational facilities. They were indeed invisible.

Bill's parents were socially conscious, as one might expect of a pastor devoted to the care and well-being of his parishioners. Bill's father was actively involved in the community, but he was apolitical, not an activist in racial matters or most other social causes. One area where he did take a more active position was in the temperance movement, which was quite logical for many people who grew up during Prohibition. Later in life, however, his father served an inner-city church in Houston.

Segregation was a fact of life, and until the end of World War II, there was little pressure for change. Indeed, blacks accepted the Jim Crow environment as their lot in life as much as the white population thought it was a natural and necessary separation of the races. Bill recalls several instances when missionaries from undeveloped countries, whom his father's church was helping to support, would stay at the church parsonage. They were devoting their lives to helping people who were economically disadvantaged. However, they were usually from Asian countries—never from Africa or even from African American communities in this country. This was the way things were—blacks in the South were just plain invisible. Occasionally, though, there were some regional black choirs that came to the church to perform. "It was the way they raised money," said Bill.

Bill's parents took a black teenager, Lucille Govan, into their home as a foster child. Bill's mother was away from home on weekdays, working as a public schoolteacher, and during the many years Lucille lived with the Olivers, she fulfilled the necessary duties of a housekeeper. Bill remembers her fondly as an equal, although others considered her to be a live-in black maid or servant. In the culture of that time and place, that was not considered unusual.

Bill Oliver's high school years were spent in Winnie, Texas, a small town of about three thousand people in Chambers County. The town was named after Fox Winnie, an engineer for the Gulf and Interstate Railway Co., who built the railroad through the area. It was settled in the late 1800s by homesteaders, and its principle agricultural crop was rice. It still hosts the Texas Rice Festival every October. In 1941, an oil field was discovered, and oil quickly became the area's major source of income. Bill recalls the constant sound of oil rigs pumping, the flames reaching into the night burning off gases, and the unmistakable smell.

Bill recalls, "I never knew where the black high school was in Winnie. Blacks were required to sit in the balcony of the local movie theater, and the whites referred to it as 'nigger heaven.' There was a black rodeo held each year in the town, and blacks would come from all over. There were buildings in town that had been housing for slaves, and they were called 'the quarters.'"

Bill was actively involved in extracurricular programs at his high school. He played several sports—track, football, tennis, and basketball. He ran the 440, did the long jump, and pole vaulted, for which he set the high school record. On one occasion, he was in a school play that was scheduled at the same time as a track meet. He juggled the conflict by pole vaulting with his actor's makeup still in place. He played halfback on the football team. His tennis doubles team made the district competition one year, but they were overpowered by the previous year's state champion, a school with a much larger enrollment. At his fiftieth high school reunion, his football coach said Bill was "one of the best athletes I ever coached."

Winnie High School had an enrollment of around one hundred students at that time. Bill was president of the student council and second in his class academically. He graduated with the highest-ranking male scholastic average and thinks he would have scored higher than the high-ranking female were it not for a C grade in band, where he played the trombone—in his own words—"not very well." He gave the graduation speech, an honor he said was somewhat expected of a preacher's kid who planned to be a preacher himself.

While in high school, he recalls attending a Methodist youth conference in Fayetteville, Arkansas, where there were a few African Americans in attendance. That was in many ways his first personal, one-on-one exposure to blacks. One of the black attendees at that conference was, several years later, also one of his classmates at divinity school. "It was probably the church programs that began to make me sensitive to the black problem, but I didn't own it until much later," Bill says. One interesting thing he recalled about this conference was the singing of "Lift Every Voice and Sing," a song considered by many to be the black national anthem.

After graduation in the summer of 1955, Bill married his high school sweetheart, Rosie Devillier. They were very young by today's standards, but filled with the enthusiasm and optimism of youth, they both enrolled at Centenary College in Shreveport, Louisiana, in the fall.

Two

COLLEGE YEARS

At that time, it was not unusual for a young man from the South who planned to enter the ministry, even at the young age of seventeen, to serve as pastor to local small churches while attending college in order to prepare for his career. It was a natural direction for a minister's son, and Bill Oliver received his license to preach from the Methodist church in 1954. He was appointed by the bishop to serve as the local pastor for three rural parishes in the villages of Scottsville, Woodlawn, and Crossroads—all in the Marshall, Texas, area. The income from these pastorates was essential for the young married man trying to pay his way through college. He conducted multiple services on weekends, moving from one

Invisible

church to the next. His education over the next year and a half came as much, or more, from his experiences as a young minister as from his courses at Centenary College in Shreveport. He remembers when he was called on to conduct his first funeral, and he was naturally anxious to do a good job. So he went to his grandfather, a minister in a Disciples of Christ church several miles distant, and asked to be given a primer on how to conduct the service.

Bill became very familiar with the Marshall area, and it was during this time that he became truly uncomfortable with a segregated environment. He recalls that up until that time, "I didn't have a great deal of consciousness about social issues." Marshall is in the northeastern corner of Texas, about forty miles from Shreveport, where Bill and his wife attended college. On weekends, Bill would make the trip to Marshall, and during the summer, he and his wife lived in a church parsonage there.

This Texas city of twenty-three thousand people at the time had developed as a railroad center and had been a political and production center of the Confederacy during the Civil War. Its black population in the 1950s was close to 40 percent, and this undoubtedly led to the sharp racial confrontations there in the 1960s.

James Farmer Jr., who became president of the Congress of Racial Equality (CORE), was a native of Marshall, and his father was president of Wiley College, an all-black educational institution in that city. James Farmer Jr. was

College Years

a member of the Wiley debating team that defeated the Harvard University team, and the film *The Great Debaters* chronicled the event. In 1905, Andrew Carnegie offered to build a library in Marshall, one of dozens of libraries he constructed across the United States. However, the city fathers insisted that it be a white-only institution. Carnegie withdrew his offer; the library was eventually built on the Wiley College campus and was open to all races.

In 1950, the Marshall Board of Censors banned the movie *Pinky* from the city because it portrayed an interracial couple. The theater manager was arrested and convicted of a misdemeanor, but the case eventually found its way to the US Supreme Court, which overturned the decision.

Residents of the Shreveport area and the Marshall area of East Texas were extremely racist, much more so than Bill Oliver had experienced in the past. He says that "Marshall, Texas, was one of the most segregated places you could imagine," and he especially found the attitudes of parishioners in those small village churches to be outwardly racist. In one instance, he was told by a parishioner that if a black person were to enter their church, "He'll never darken the door of this church again." Bill also recalls registering for the military draft in 1955 in Marshall, and the clerk said to him, "Don't worry; you won't be picked." Later, he became certain the insinuation was that the registrar had a way to replace a white draftee's name with that of a young black man.

Centenary College was a Methodist school, and Bill was given a "preacher boy scholarship." However, he found the environment at Centenary equally as prejudiced and racist as Marshall, Texas. "The local newspaper, the *Shreveport Journal*, was openly racist." One of the fraternities even paraded around in Confederate uniforms, and it was common to see Confederate flags in dormitory rooms. He said the attitude was that the Civil War was not over; it was just in recess. "After one and a half years, I'd had enough," he said. So Bill and his wife left the college and the Marshall area and moved back to the southeastern corner of the state where they had grown up.

By that time, his first child, Rene, had been born. He took another pastorate at a church in the town of Devers, Texas, several miles west of the city of Beaumont. There were no racial incidents while he was at this church, and although civil rights was becoming a national issue, "racial discrimination was not talked about openly." He enrolled at Lamar State College of Technology, now Lamar University, in Beaumont, and he continued to pursue a bachelor's degree. All through his college years, Bill's ultimate goal was to get a bachelor's degree so he could then attend a theological seminary.

After only one semester at Lamar, he transferred to the University of Houston. Even though it was a

College Years

one-and-a-half-hour drive from his pastorate in Devers, the curriculum was much broader and allowed him to major in philosophy, a logical major for someone who was to attend a seminary. He was able to arrange his schedule so that he did not have to commute to Houston every day. To the extent allowed by his busy schedule, he participated in extracurricular activities, including being president of the Methodist church student organization at the university.

The University of Houston at this time had an enrollment of about twenty thousand students, but no African Americans. Bill's second child, Cecile, was born during the two years that he attended the university. Bill graduated in 1959 with a major in philosophy and a minor in theater, and that fall he entered the Perkins School of Theology at Southern Methodist University.

Three

Divinity School at SMU

As he entered the Perkins Seminary after four years of college, Bill's original intention of becoming a minister and preacher had changed. He, of course, planned to get his theology degree but thought he would then become a teacher. Even so, in order to support his family, he took on another Methodist pastorate in Oakwood, Texas, south of Dallas and University Park, the location of SMU. In June of 1960, the bishop of the Methodist church formally made him a deacon, a position that allowed him to perform more of the duties of an ordained minister.

After the birth of their second child, Cecile, Bill's wife, Rosie, began to spend more and more time back in

Divinity School at SMU

Winnie, Texas, with her parents. He says, "I was naïve about my marital situation. I didn't know the marriage was in trouble." During his first year at seminary, his wife and children spent even more time back in Winnie. Although they did not become legally divorced until 1962, they had effectively become separated. He was immersed in divinity school, and gradually his sensitivity to racial issues was emerging.

Throughout 1960, the civil rights movement gained increased momentum across the United States. As is frequently the case, much of this momentum for change was occurring on college and university campuses. Even in some southern states, college students were demonstrating through sit-ins, attempting to open up public accommodations, especially restaurants. Sit-ins at a university in Greensboro, North Carolina, received national attention and began to have a ripple effect in other universities. At the time, SMU had only a token number of black students, and Bill Oliver said the university "was minimally sensitive to social issues."

Close to the SMU campus was the University Drug Store, frequented by students, and it had a busy, but segregated, lunch counter where no blacks were served. In the spring of 1960, a group of SMU students, including Bill and one black classmate, decided to stage a sit-in. The black was refused service at the counter, and the other students refused to leave unless the black was served. This standoff lasted for some period of time and was followed by a second sit-in, after which the drug store closed its doors and never again reopened. The students had been sprayed with DDT, and some believed the food and goods in the store had been contaminated by the insecticide. The incident received considerable press attention. It was Bill Oliver's first sit-in, and the first outward demonstration of his feelings about racial injustice. When asked, "What caused you to get involved at that time?" he simply answered, "I thought it was the right thing to do." During the following several decades, there would be dozens of additional situations where he vocally and physically confronted injustice and discrimination, not only racial, but economic, gender, and social injustices of many different kinds.

In the summer and fall of 1960, Bill became an active volunteer in John F. Kennedy's campaign for president. He went door to door in the Dallas area, trying to convince people to vote for JFK and reassuring the primarily Baptist neighborhoods that JFK's Roman Catholic religion was not a factor in his qualifications for president. The Texas campaign organizers felt that his being a Protestant seminary student would give Bill strong credibility in making this argument. It was also his first introduction to the power of computers. The computer printout that directed him to the right houses to call on was sorted by various demographic factors such as race, political affiliation, religion, and specific location of each house. This initial introduction to computers and their ability to identify select groupings of people would later play a significant role in his planning and organizing efforts to confront injustice.

During the campaign, he and a seminary classmate attended a JFK rally when the candidate was in Dallas. They arrived early and worked their way up to the large press section at the front of the auditorium. It was an exciting day for a young person who saw hope and the possibility of significant change in an administration of a youthful and vibrant leader with liberal ideals. The two seminary students were the only ones in the press section to stand and cheer enthusiastically upon the arrival of the candidate. They feared they might be removed as a result of their exuberance. At the conclusion of Kennedy's speech, Bill actually jumped up on the stage and pushed past the then Texas Governor John Connolly and Speaker of the House Sam Rayburn to get closer to the future president. At the conclusion of the event, the two enthusiastic students took a large Vote for Kennedy poster back to the school and placed it in an attic window. It stayed there for several days for the entire student body to see.

When asked, "Who were the most influential people in your life?" Bill quickly listed Rev. Dr. W. B. J. Martin, a professor at Perkins, as the person having the most impact. He was a Welshman, a minister, and a professor who taught preaching at the Perkins Seminary. Bill has said, "He was my mentor." Rev. Dr. Martin came to this country as a Fulbright Scholar and remained here until his death. Prior to taking the position at Perkins, he had been the chaplain at the University of Edinburgh in Scotland.

Bill spent many hours with Rev. Dr. Martin inside and outside of the classroom, discussing numerous subjects, and it is obvious that this minister had a profound impact on Bill's spiritual beliefs. It was through this association that Bill abandoned his idea of teaching and reverted back to a career goal of becoming a minister. Rev. Dr. Martin convinced him that a "parish ministry gives you freedom. In the church, you can disagree without being disagreeable," adding, "People have a right to self-determination" in their religious beliefs.

When asked about his theological beliefs, Bill makes several statements underscoring the fact he had developed a more liberal philosophy. He says, "Theology is life. There are no absolutes. I'm not a literalist. If your beliefs are holding you down, then you've got to change. People should be liberated from what oppresses them. The church should be a liberator. Theology is anthropology."

By that time, Bill had become disillusioned with the Methodist church. The southern Methodist churches were segregated, with separate white and black churches, and even held separate state and regional conferences. He left the pastorate of the Oakwood church and became associate minister of the First Community Congregational Church in Dallas, where the senior minister of the church was his mentor, Rev. Dr. Martin. This church was very influential in the Dallas community, and in fact, Rev. Dr. Martin had been chosen to give the invocation at the gathering that never occurred on the day President Kennedy was assassinated.

The national Congregational Christian Church denomination went through a merger with the Evangelical and Reformed Church in the late 1950s and became the United Church of Christ (UCC). Similar to the Congregational Church, the new merged denomination had no hierarchical structure of control over its churches; each church was independent. Each local church owned its own buildings, recruited and hired its own clergy, could choose to leave the UCC denomination at any time, and answered to no higher authority than God.

Significant for Bill, the Congregational Church historically had played an important role in many southern states after the Civil War. It established dozens of schools for blacks, and some eventually became black colleges that still exist today. They include Fisk, Huston-Tillotson, Tougaloo, Tuskegee, Dillard, and Talladega. The Congregational Church also established several black churches as outreach or mission churches, and the national organization supported them financially until they became self-sufficient.

In the spring of 1963, before his graduation from Perkins, Bill was ordained as a minister of the United Church of Christ.

The civil rights March on Washington, where Dr. Martin Luther King Jr. delivered his famous "I Have a Dream" speech on the steps of the Lincoln Memorial, occurred in August of 1963. The NAACP in Dallas chartered a bus to travel to Austin to hold a march and demonstration at the state capitol, coinciding with the Washington, D.C., event. Bill Oliver was still residing in Dallas and joined the group traveling to Austin. The gathering of some ten thousand people was a coalition of individuals representing labor unions, blacks, Spanish-speaking people, and liberal democrats.

Bill was asked, on the spur of the moment, to speak at the gathering. Being a white minister, as well as a native Texan, he would be perceived as a person with credibility that civil rights activists from the North did not have. There was a pervasive belief on the part of many southerners that the civil rights movement was being fueled by northern Yankee troublemakers. Bill agreed to speak, even though he had nothing prepared.

He called upon his ministerial training and a sermon he had recently preached at the First Congregational Church in Dallas. When I asked Bill what he spoke about, he said, "The church's dry rot." The *Dallas Times Herald* reported on the demonstration and quoted Bill directly from his remarks, "Unless the church is alive to the issues of the day, it will not be with us long." Not only were churches in the South segregated, but across the country as well, and even today, the statement that "the one-hour church service on Sunday mornings may be the most segregated hour in the week" continues to be true.

Bill states that his speech at that Austin demonstration "propelled me into a position of being one of the leaders of liberal politics in Texas for the next twenty years." Although he is recognized for his active pursuit of racial justice, over the next two decades, he also became an active force in Texas politics.

Four

The Call to The Plymouth Church

With his graduation from the Perkins School of Theology Bill began his search for employment, buoyed by the confidence of his mentor, Dr. Martin, and his growing sensitivity to racial injustice. He researched several opportunities around the country and noticed one from a UCC Congregational church in Beaumont, Texas. He was familiar with this city, which was located not far from the town of Winnie, where his children lived and where he had gone to high school. The Plymouth United Church of Christ in Beaumont was a small, predominantly black church, although Bill was not initially aware of this, and it had been established in 1919 by the Homeland Mission Board of the Congregational Church.

The church's original pastor, Rev. Charles Graham, an African American, had held the position for more than twenty years, and in fact the church was known as the Graham Congregational Church until the summer of 1963. After Rev. Graham died in 1943, the church was served by part-time pastors.

Bill met with the moderator of the church, Dr. Laddie Melton, who was the son of the first member of the church in 1919. Dr. Melton also happened to be Andrew Young Jr's great uncle. This connection with the future US congressman from Texas, mayor of Atlanta, and United Nations ambassador began a relationship that significantly impacted Bill's involvement and activism in civil rights over the next several years. Andy Young was on Dr. Martin Luther King's staff at that time and was himself an ordained UCC minister who preached at least three times at the Plymouth Church while Bill was pastor.

Bill preached a sermon to the Beaumont congregation on his initial visit, and then, a few weeks later, he received a call to become its pastor. He chose this church over other possible positions, including a church in an affluent New Jersey community. It was most unusual at that time for a young Caucasian raised in the South to become a minister of a black church anywhere in the United States, but especially in the Deep South. His appointment received considerable media coverage throughout Texas, and the Houston and Beaumont press even carried a one-year follow-up article on Bill's pastorate.

The church was still partially financially supported by the UCC Board of Homeland Ministies, working toward the time when it would be entirely self-sufficient. Bill was very concerned that this church not be thought of as a mission church. He did not want to be seen as a missionary coming in "to tell the people what to do and what they had to believe."

One significant factor that influenced Bill to accept the call was that this church had a history of active involvement in the community. Black UCC churches tended to be more liberal and forward looking than other black churches. They looked out beyond their church walls, encouraged education, and practiced an outreach ministry. Most other black churches during the time were still victims of the Jim Crow environment: "go along and get along." However, over the years, the Plymouth UCC Congregational Church had organized a YMCA, a day-care center, Boy Scout and Girl Scout troops, a medical clinic and hospital, and also a newspaper—all for blacks, who were excluded from these white organizations and facilities in Beaumont. It is significant that even the need for a social worker in the city of Beaumont was first recognized by the church, who then hired one several years before Bill's arrival.

Under Bill's guidance and leadership, the Plymouth Church would continue this type of ministry during his twenty-three years as pastor. They built a large housing facility that was federally funded by Housing and Urban Development (HUD) and included a playground for black children on the church grounds. Bill says, "I saw this opportunity as a real challenge, even if I only lasted a year." Serving any congregation more than twenty years was very unusual for any Protestant denomination, considering the average pastorate was usually less than six or seven years. Especially through the tumultuous times of the 1960s and 1970s, this longevity speaks volumes about the love and respect he enjoyed from his congregation.

Before accepting the call, however, Bill visited his father, who was in a hospital at the time, to inform him about his decision to go to the Beaumont church. His father expressed concern over the dangers and physical risks but then said to Bill, "I could see it coming!"

The church's congregation was more educated and affluent than the typical black church in Beaumont, and its membership covered the spectrum, including professionals, professors from Lamar University, and business people, along with welfare mothers. A Mobil Oil plant manager was one of the church members. The broad mixture of members, their more liberal outlook, and the active support and involvement of the congregation would be significant factors in Bill's civil rights activities during his ministry.

Today, Lamar University in Beaumont, a state institution, has a student enrollment of fifteen thousand; however, it was only a third that size in 1963. The university had removed its racial barriers only two years earlier, but at the time still had only a handful of black students, and significantly, the school facilities were still segregated, including the school's library. Some of the school's faculty, and many of its students, as well as members of Bill's church, became active participants in marches and sit-ins in support of racial justice.

Beaumont was a city of one hundred twenty thousand in 1963 and had a large black population; however, only two members of the city's police force were black. It was an oil city, with more than one hundred refineries and petrochemical plants. The first discovery of oil in Texas, in the 1930s, was the Spindle Top oil field in Beaumont. The oil industry was so large that there were oil camps where many of the workers lived.

The Ku Klux Klan (KKK) was strong and active, especially in the rural areas around Beaumont. The small town of Vidor, a short distance from Beaumont, was considered by many to be the area's KKK center, and it even boasted a KKK bookstore. Racial discrimination and the

Jim Crow environment were deeply embedded in both the white and black cultures.

In June of 1943, there were serious race riots that received national attention and required state and federal law enforcement organizations to quell the uprising. Following an accusation of assault on a white woman, close to four thousand whites marched on city hall and demanded action, even though the white woman could not identify the supposed offender. The crowd dispersed into smaller groups and terrorized black neighborhoods. Stores, restaurants, and homes were ransacked, more than one hundred homes were set on fire, and many blacks were assaulted. More than two hundred were arrested, at least fifty were injured, and three blacks and one white eventually died. Martial law was declared by the Texas governor, and the National Guard, state police, and Texas Rangers were all called in. A curfew was established, public gatherings were forbidden, and blacks were not allowed to go to work. All of this activity occurred in and around the neighborhood of the Graham Congregational Church.

The riots resulted from tensions that had their roots in World War II. Beaumont, a port city on the Sabine River and only ten miles from the Gulf of Mexico, had become a major shipbuilding and petrochemical center during the war. The rapid population growth brought about some forced integration, since municipal facilities were not adequate to permit complete segregation.

Housing shortages were severe, the races were forced to live in close proximity, and blacks began to have access to semiskilled and skilled jobs that put them in competition with whites. Tensions grew as the population increased, and there were even some food shortages. With this growing turmoil, the head of the federal regional food administration warned Washington that the situation was "conducive to riot." To fuel the volatile situation further, the Ku Klux Klan had planned a regional convention in Beaumont for late June 1943. Similar to most public protests and riots, there was more than one factor that caused the upheaval.

There was a subsequent riot in 1948; however, it was not as serious. These two events left the city, and especially many in the black population, fearful of any incidents that might again spark hatred and violence. This backdrop tended to underscore the hesitancy of many leaders in the black community to take a leadership, or even visible, role in civil rights activities in the 1960s.

The Beaumont public schools were minimally integrated in 1963, with only a few black students in the system. Bill said, "They tried to find any way to argue that they were legal—separate but equal." The separate black and white schools were finally merged in the 1970s, and Bill was involved in the integration efforts throughout the 1960s and 1970s.

The Call to The Plymouth Church

This was the environment in which Bill Oliver accepted the position as pastor of a liberal African American church, during that volatile period of the national movement for social justice and civil rights in 1963. Different from the Methodist church hierarchical structure, where a bishop assigns its pastors, Bill emphasized, "I was their choice, not the choice of a bishop."

And so a young, southern, white pastor assumed the ministry of a black church in East Texas that generated significant press coverage in Dallas, Houston, and Philadelphia. One of the articles was written by a young staff writer for the *Dallas Times Herald*, Jim Lehrer, who later earned national prominence as the news anchor for *PBS News Hour* and as a moderator of presidential debates.

Bill has said, "I had to go through a learning process in 1963 and 1964. I had to learn how blacks survived. I really didn't have a great deal of consciousness about social issues."

Bill's father and grandfather participated in his installation as pastor of the Plymouth UCC Congregational Church, and his friend and mentor, Rev. Dr. W. B. J. Martin from the Perkins Seminary, gave the installation sermon.

Five

First Year as Pastor in Beaumont

Bill assumed his responsibilities as pastor of the Plymouth Congregational Church on September 1, 1963. It was a tumultuous time for the civil rights movement across the South, and the news of numerous racial events captured national and international attention. Medgar Evers, a civil rights activist, had been murdered in Jackson, Mississippi in June 1963. The March on Washington and Dr. Martin Luther King Jr.'s "I Have a Dream" speech occurred in August 1963. The bombing of the Sixteenth Street Baptist Church in Birmingham, Alabama, where four young girls were killed, occurred on September 15, 1963. President Kennedy was assassinated

First Year as Pastor in Beaumont

in Dallas, Texas, in November 1963. Federal legislation that became known as the Civil Rights Act of 1964 was working its way through Congress. Demonstrations, marches, and sit-ins in support of this legislation were occurring throughout the southern states, and in northern cities such as Detroit, there were also racial demonstrations. Even though these sit-ins were nonviolent actions, they frequently generated violent reactions from the white community and local and state law enforcement.

Bill Oliver was thrown into this environment in the city of Beaumont, and he quickly became involved in numerous attempts to integrate public accommodations through sit-ins and demonstrations, as he also became educated on the issue of voter disenfranchisement.

Shortly after arriving in the city, he attended an NAACP meeting and met a local man, Albert J. Price, who became Bill's closest friend over the years and who he has said was one of those individuals who had a major influence on his life. In addition to their involvement and commitment to civil rights causes over those years, they became fierce competitors at the game of chess. Bill said, "Initially I was beaten badly at every game, but after a while I was holding my own. When I got to win more frequently, Al lost interest, and the frequency of games slowed down."

Al was a native of Beaumont, the son of a black Baptist minister, and was well known and respected in the black community. He had recently retired as a captain and one of the few black pilots in the Strategic Air Command, the branch of the US Air Force that flew large bombers and carried nuclear weapons. He was anxious to become a commercial airline pilot, and he eventually became one of a handful of black pilots with American Airlines. His picture was on the cover of *JET Magazine* in 1967.

Later, as a result of Bill's forceful encouragement, Al Price ran unsuccessfully for the Texas legislature several times, but then in 1976 became the first black to be elected to that legislature from East Texas since Reconstruction. Al Price had finally won as a result of Bill organizing aggressive voter-registration activities, and in fact Bill had played a major role in redrawing the legislative district. He and Bill were so close that some of Al's political opponents claimed he was under the influence of a white pastor. Representative Price served in that capacity for twenty years, and Bill served as his campaign manager for several of his elections. Along the way, Al became active in the World Council of Churches and eventually became a member of its Central Committee. An article in the *Beaumont Enterprise* at the time of his death in 2012 said the following:

> "Al Price was known for fighting for civil rights, inspiring others and for his fierce commitment to helping the underdog.

First Year as Pastor in Beaumont

> But relatives and friends remembered him as fun loving, knowledgeable and brutally honest—with just the right amount of humor to remove the sting."

The article went on to quote the Beaumont Independent School District Superintendent:

> "He was what I call a true hero. He was not only a hero, but an officer and a gentleman."

Later in their friendship, Bill Oliver officiated at Al Price's wedding, and several years later, Al served as the best man at Bill's wedding.

An official from the Board of Homeland Ministries of the UCC, the church organization that was providing some financial support for the Plymouth Church, came to visit Bill shortly after he became its pastor. Bill was naturally a little apprehensive about the visit, being a new minister, and wondered what the church's reaction would be to his civil rights activities. They discussed the racial environment in Beaumont, and Bill's mind was greatly relieved when, on the way to the airport at the conclusion of the visit, the official asked him, "Why haven't you gone to jail?" Without specifically saying so, Bill understood that such an event would probably be supported. Over the next few years, he was arrested on several occasions and spent several nights in jail, all in support of social justice causes.

In the fall of 1963, Bill and Al worked together to organize boycotts and sit-ins to force integration of restaurants and other public accommodations. Bill was first arrested at that time, along with several of his church members, including students from his church youth group as young as fifth and sixth graders. Along with Lamar University students, they were arrested for conducting a sit-in at a local restaurant and then refusing to leave until they were served. This incident received considerable coverage in the local Beaumont press and was followed shortly by other sit-ins and boycotts at other restaurants.

On a subsequent occasion, at a sit-in at another restaurant, thirty-four demonstrators, including Bill, were arrested and kept in the police station over a Saturday night. "We were scared to death. We didn't know what was going to happen to us, and I had all these young people along with me." As a result, when his congregation showed up at his church for the Sunday-morning service, there was no minister to conduct the service and give the sermon. The members left the church and went to the police station, where they sang freedom songs outside the city jail. The demonstrators were finally released on Monday morning. Bill becomes very emotional when he relates this incident and the spontaneous support he received from his congregation.

One incident involved the annual Jefferson County Fair in Beaumont in October 1963. It had always been a segregated event, and blacks were only allowed to attend on one day that was called "Negro Day." Prior to the opening of the fair, Bill and a group of black leaders, including Al Price, made the city and fair officials aware that if they did not open up the fair to blacks for the entire week, there would be a large demonstration at the fairgrounds on opening day. Although some black leaders opposed the threat of a demonstration, not wanting to rock the boat in race relations, there were several well-known and respected black community leaders who supported the effort to remove the racial barrier. The police warned, "It's going to get out of control. Remember the riots in the forties." Meetings and discussions took place behind the scenes over several days, and the officials finally agreed to integrate the event, but only thirty minutes before the fair was scheduled to open.

Bill would say, "Boycotts are all about money. You get in their pocketbooks and it affects their minds." During this period in late 1963 and early 1964, it became evident that some Beaumont restaurants wanted to take down the racial barriers but were reluctant to be the first to make the move. The Chamber of Commerce wanted a resolution, and some restaurant owners were pressing the chamber to take a stand. The local restaurant association finally voted to desegregate. Many in the community, both black and white, still remembered the race riots in the 1940s and were fearful of the demonstrations and boycotts that might trigger new riots.

As a result of the demonstrations and sit-ins, Beaumont restaurants were desegregated two months before the Civil Rights Act of 1964 was passed by the US Congress and signed into law by President Johnson.

With each of these events, Bill's education into the realities of racial discrimination resulted in his steady evolution as an activist, and by the end of his first year in Beaumont, he became recognized as a leader in the civil rights movement in East Texas. The fact that he was a native son of East Texas contradicted the widely held belief that "these civil rights problems are the result of northern Yankees coming down here and stirring up trouble." Bill has said, "My activities caused me to lose old friends, even friends from seminary. It was like I had some contagious disease!" The local police chief accused him and a local rabbi of being communists, a convenient label at the time for anyone who disagreed with local authorities and was looking for change.

During October of 1963, Bill attended a UCC Homeland Ministries meeting in New Orleans with Rev. Andrew Young. Rev. Young was an ordained UCC minister, a member of Dr. Martin Luther King Jr.'s staff, and his activities with the Southern Christian Leadership Conference (SCLC) were partially financially supported by the Homeland Ministries board. Dr. King and the SCLC worked primarily through churches for their support. While at this meeting, Bill and Andy attended a civil rights meeting at a restaurant in Plaquemines Parish, Louisiana, an area that was experiencing significant violence in reaction to various civil rights activities. There had been threats and beatings in the area by the Ku Klux Klan, and law enforcement tended to look the other way. Group gatherings were dangerous. Several of the blacks attending the meeting wore bandages from physical beatings. Bill becomes emotional when describing this meeting, and would later say, "I came to realize that some people were prepared to die for the cause." He recalls the gathering singing a freedom song with the words "This may be the last time we sing together." He says, "To me it had just been a song in the past, but to them, the words were real. It was a whole new world to me."

As his activities and visibility grew, the United Church of Christ conference minister in Texas wanted to have Bill removed as minister of the Plymouth Church. He wanted to "rein me in and stop the funding." The executive director for Church Life of the UCC, Rev. Reuben Shears, an African American himself, came to Beaumont and reassured Bill of his position. Rev. Shears later became the pastor of the largest UCC church in

Invisible

the country, the Trinity Church in Chicago. Many years later, he would attend a recognition dinner in Beaumont honoring Bill.

On several occasions throughout these early months in Beaumont, Bill tried to visit his two children, who were still living in the town of Winnie. However, when he reached the town, he was not allowed to see them. In fact, they had been purposefully moved. The divorce had been finalized. He did not contest it, and their mother had been given custody. Subsequently, Bill's first wife remarried, and when her new husband adopted the two children, they assumed his name. Bill was not notified in advance of the adoption proceedings. His oldest daughter was five at the time, and it would be several decades before he would see her again. He has still been unable to make contact with his youngest daughter. He has said, "We were too young when we got married." However, it seems as though one of the factors in both the divorce and the forced separation from his children was his civil rights activities and the press coverage that specifically identified Bill as a local and visible civil rights leader.

Six

THE CIVIL RIGHTS AND VOTING RIGHTS ACTS

In a narrative résumé written many years after leaving Beaumont, Bill Oliver wrote the following:

"My pastorate in Beaumont provided some of the most exciting and unique opportunities anyone could imagine in the last half of the twentieth century. The congregation had a history of involvement in working for change on behalf of its people, and indeed all people. The church made it possible for me to be free to pursue my ministry in ways only few have had a chance at."

The Civil Rights Act of 1964 was signed into law in July. It was landmark legislation that made it unlawful to discriminate based upon race, as well as ethnicity and religion. Bill, along with several church, union, and liberal political officials, sent a telegram to President Johnson after President Kennedy's assassination, demanding he support the legislation that had yet to be passed by Congress. At the time, there was great concern that Johnson would not place his considerable influence behind passage of the bill. When the vote was finally taken, Congressman Jack Brooks from the Beaumont district demonstrated his personal courage as the only Texas congressman to vote for the bill. Although under that law all public accommodations had to be integrated, it did not occur overnight, and in some cases not for many years. Public demonstrations and sit-ins continued to be staged in order to force compliance with the new federal law.

In most black communities, it was the older adults who were reluctant—even fearful—to participate in integration activities, but in Bill's church, the older people were supportive of the efforts of its youth and their demonstrations to bring racial justice. As a result of his friendship with Andrew Young, Bill arranged to have

The Civil Rights and Voting Rights Acts

student volunteers come to Beaumont and give instruction in nonviolent techniques. The four Southern Christian Leadership Conference workers lived in the church parsonage for two months and trained residents in the nonviolent philosophy of Dr. Martin Luther King Jr.

The leader of the SCLC group was a young woman, Elizabeth Hayes, who had left college to work with the SCLC. The training was more than just words; it taught behavior when faced with violence or the threat of violence. They were told not to carry any kind of knife, letter opener, or nail file for fear those items might be used as an excuse for police action. Detailed planning was essential before any sit-in activity. It was important to count the number of seats in a restaurant, the number of steps to an exit, and establish a lookout to be alert to any violence. They were trained how to protect the female demonstrators and were careful to exclude any individuals who had aggressive personalities. Bill says that anyone who preferred a violent approach "stayed back and made sandwiches."

The Lamar University students and some of its faculty became increasingly involved in desegregation efforts. As the process moved along with successes, there was increased support from blacks in other churches, but interestingly not from their pastors. It was the ingrained go along to get along attitude. The pastor of a local black Baptist church said, "The SCLC is not welcome in this church." In one instance, a Catholic priest who did become involved was quickly moved to another diocese.

Throughout this time, efforts increased in the southern states to combat voter disenfranchisement of blacks, and much of the specific SCLC training involved efforts to increase the number of black voters. Freedom Summer occurred in 1964 and involved hundreds of volunteers, many of them northern college white students who spent that summer working to register blacks. Although the original registration efforts focused specifically on abuses in the state of Mississippi, there were clear violations in many other states, including Texas. African Americans were systematically kept from registering because of expensive poll taxes, and in many instances, complicated literacy tests. During the course of that summer, there were several activists killed in Mississippi, both whites and blacks, and dozens of people arrested.

Andrew Young related to Bill a specific incident when he went to Greenwood, Mississippi, bringing bail money to get the release of an SCLC worker, Annelle Ponder, who had been jailed for bringing blacks to register to vote. Rev. Young was shocked to find she had been severely beaten and her face bloodied and bruised. Through her swollen lips, she said one word, "Freedom!"

After the SCLC volunteers had worked several weeks in Beaumont, Bill arranged for them to conduct training

The Civil Rights and Voting Rights Acts

with some labor unions around the state. The unions had become an important factor in voter registration in Texas, primarily because they needed the black vote to advance their own political agenda, specifically wage and working-condition issues. These training sessions were set up in black neighborhoods. At that time, there were separate black and white unions, but some white union groups supported integration efforts, again for their own specific economic reasons.

Bill was a life member of NAACP and became a key volunteer in the voter-registration efforts of the organization, serving on the board of directors of local branches for more than thirty years. The state of Texas had imposed a poll tax during Reconstruction after the Civil War that discouraged many blacks from registering. In addition, the Democratic primary in the state of Texas was a whites-only primary until 1948, when it was declared unconstitutional. Since the state was overwhelmingly Democrat, the winner in the primaries was easily the victor in the main election. Blacks had been effectively excluded from the electoral process. The process of registering the disenfranchised voter after 1948 proved to be a long and tedious one, continuing for several decades.

When Bill arrived in Beaumont in 1963, nongovernment organizations (NGOs) were permitted to sign up people and collect the poll tax. Bill's church became active and aggressive in "selling poll taxes." They would help people fill out the registration applications, collect the poll tax fee, and then forward the money and the form to the city or county. The Southern Christian Leadership Conference provided some of the funds necessary to help accomplish these goals. Bill subsequently served as the Texas representative for the SCLC, attending several regional and national meetings.

The Voting Rights Act was then under discussion in Congress. Publicity for Freedom Summer, and especially the violence in Mississippi, had gained national attention. The murders of Michael Schwerner, James Chaney, and Andrew Goodman in June of 1964 captured the emotion of the country like nothing else had up to that time in the civil rights movement. They were all working for the Congress of Racial Equality (CORE) in the state of Mississippi. Bill believes this act galvanized President Johnson to get behind the bill. He says, "It was the end of the feds sitting on their hands."

The Selma to Montgomery, Alabama, march in March of 1965 was a response to the violence that grew out of voter-registration efforts over several years in the city of Selma. The SCLC had a strong presence in the area, and following the murder of one of the protestors, it organized the march from Selma to Montgomery to confront Governor George Wallace about voter-registration abuses and the need for the state to protect the rights of demonstrators. The SCLC carefully planned the tactics

The Civil Rights and Voting Rights Acts

for demonstrations, including where and when they would be most effective. The previous public racist statements and actions of Bull Connor, the Birmingham commissioner of public safety, and Governor George Wallace necessitated a well-planned strategy for the march. The organizers had learned they had to create an opportunity for people across the nation to see on television and in photos what was happening.

As the march proceeded over several days and gained increasing press coverage, more and more people became involved. Bill Oliver and one of his parishioners joined the march during its last two days, and when it reached the foot of the capitol steps in Montgomery, the number had grown to twenty-five thousand people. Bill's parishioner, an older black member of his congregation, said to Bill, "I've never done anything before." Bill became emotional relating the event and said the man carried the Texas state flag and sang, "The Eyes of Texas Are Upon You."

Bill says the tension of the marchers increased as they turned up Dexter Avenue in Montgomery toward the state house. There were large numbers of whites on the sidewalks yelling obscenities at the marchers; however, during the week-long march, more and more whites had actually joined in the demonstration. Bill says his principle fear was being shot by a sniper from a window in one of the taller buildings in the city.

Invisible

At the conclusion of the march, Bill and his friend left Montgomery, and as they headed away on Highway 80 back to Selma, they came across a large police presence. Bill decided to use discretion, quickly reversing direction and heading south toward Mobile, then west toward Beaumont on a more southerly route. Later, he learned that a white woman from Detroit who had participated in the march was murdered a short distance from where Bill had turned around. Many southerners continued to claim that the demonstrators were all northern troublemakers.

In July of 1965, Bill was a key player in several demonstrations in Huntsville, Texas. He would later say one of them was the most dangerous civil rights demonstration he experienced, and one where he feared for his life.

Several black Huntsville high school students had attended an AFL-CIO interracial conference in Austin earlier in the summer. When they returned home, they were motivated to pressure the city for school integration and equal treatment in job opportunities. They formed an organization called the Huntsville Action Youth (HA-YOU), which was affiliated with the Southern Christian Leadership Conference. Since a large percentage of blacks lived in Walker County, they would have a significant impact on elections once they were registered. At that time, Bill Oliver was the Texas representative for the SCLC, and the organization sent two workers to Huntsville to help organize the students. Sit-ins and

The Civil Rights and Voting Rights Acts

demonstrations, even after the Civil Rights Act of 1964, were still necessary to break down the segregation of restaurants and theaters and to encourage voter registration. The nonviolent demonstrations in Huntsville were spread over several days and were eventually met with physical abuse and arrests by the police. The state police and the Texas Rangers were called in to control the demonstrations and assist the local police.

At the height of the demonstrations, Bill and more than two dozen young African Americans were arrested for refusing to disperse. The Texas Rangers were the elite unit of the state police and were known and feared for their use of unreasonable physical force. Bill and an African American SCLC demonstrator, B. T. Bonner, were singled out from the group and dragged through the streets to the jail. Bill's clothes were torn, worn through, and stained with blood. He states that at one point he heard a ranger say, "Block the streets while we do to these guys what we gotta do." Bill relates he was worried for his family should something happen to him. "The fear of not knowing what the final outcome would be was constantly on my mind as I was being dragged along."

While being dragged, Bill noticed the FBI agent he had met with earlier that afternoon, Bob Wyde, sitting in a car beside the road. He said, "Hi, Bob." The FBI was documenting events as they occurred in the South, and it was common practice for civil rights organizers to notify them before they held a demonstration. Bill believes his greeting to the FBI agent was noticed by the rangers, and that may well have saved him from serious physical harm, or even death. Later that evening, a newly returned Vietnam veteran rallied together more than a hundred other protestors—blacks and whites, men and women, adults and children, young and old—and they marched past the armed rangers and police to sit on the jailhouse steps throughout the night, singing freedom songs. Bill was finally released from jail after the UCC Board of Homeland Ministry put up a bond of two hundred fifty dollars. He was charged with disturbing the peace, and was eventually convicted of unlawful assembly and, of all things, restraint of trade.

President Johnson had said that the solution to racism was political. The political consensus became clear after all of these events throughout the South received national attention. This growing public outrage was critical to the voting-rights legislation moving forward, which was finally approved by congress and signed by the president in August of 1965.

During the fall of 1965, Bill Oliver married Loretta Williams, a young African American from Beaumont. She had been the secretary for the voter-registration effort at the church, and was also a student at Lamar University. Because of the racist environment at the time, it was not possible for Bill and Loretta to have a normal courtship out in the open. Interracial marriage, miscegenation, was a violation of Texas law at the time, and violators were subject to a fifteen-year prison sentence. Not until 1967 did the Supreme Court do away with miscegenation, in the case of Loving v. Virginia. Both Bill's and Loretta's parents were opposed to the marriage, fearful of the risks of violating the accepted culture, especially during a time of racial upheaval. Some of Bill's friends said he and Loretta should move up north for their own safety. Bill called the state attorney general's office to inform them of his intention to marry Loretta, and the official said, "I won't help you, but I won't prevent you." In effect, he was saying he would look the other way.

Bill says he and Loretta took both sets of parents to see the film *Guess Who's Coming to Dinner*, in which Sidney Poitier portrayed the lead character who wanted to marry the daughter of a white family. He says, "We spent the entire film looking at our parents, not the movie." Loretta's parents were so upset with the marriage that they had no contact with their daughter for more than a year. Bill said, "Love sometimes flies in the face of reason." Subsequently, the relationship was mended, and Bill had a close relationship with her parents, perhaps solidified by his mother-in-law's cooking. He said, "She made the best cornbread ever."

Bill and Loretta could not get a marriage license in Beaumont, so they found an official two hundred fifty miles away, in San Antonio, who was willing to take the risk and issue the license. Bill approached one of his friends, a black pastor, to officiate at the marriage. The minister told him he could not and said, "My head's in the mouth of the alligator." He was referring to the fact that his church had only recently taken out a mortgage with a local bank. Another black pastor without such misgivings conducted the service. On their wedding day three shots were fired into the church parsonage. Bill learned years later from an FBI source that the Ku Klux Klan had threatened action in Galveston County at a cottage where they spent their wedding night. Their marriage was statewide news.

Interestingly, in an environment where many older members of the Beaumont community, both black and white, were opposed to interracial marriage, either from prejudice or fear of the risks, younger people were more supportive. One example is that after their marriage Loretta was elected president of her sorority at Lamar University.

During their marriage, Loretta would give birth to two sons: William (Bill) Oliver IV, in 1967, and David, in 1970. After almost twenty years of marriage, Bill and Loretta divorced in the 1980s, and Bill states, "I guess we just grew apart." Was this a second instance where his commitment to his ministry and his committed involvement as a civil rights activist, perhaps to the frequent exclusion of this family, gradually eroded their relationship?

Rev. Willaim B. Oliver, Jr.

Rev. Dr. William B. Oliver

Rosie Devillier Oliver

Graham Congregational
Church—Beaumont, Texas

THE DALLAS TIMES HERALD

City News

Monday, Sept. 2, 1963 ★★★ A—25

'COME ALIVE,' CHURCH TOLD

Minister Explains Reasons For Taking Negro Pastorate

By JIM LEHRER
Staff Writer

A young Congregational minister who will become pastor of an all-Negro church in Beaumont this week has expressed the hope that the church "will not be a Rip Van Winkle who sleeps through a revolution."

The Rev. William B. Oliver III delivered his last sermon Sunday morning at the First Community Church of Dallas (Congregational), United Church of Christ, where he has been associate minister for two years.

He takes over as full-time pastor of the Negro Graham Congregational Church in Beaumont on Tuesday.

The 28-year-old minister began his sermon by asking: "Why should I choose at a reduction of salary, to go to a church that has only 28 members, a dilapidated building, and in the inner city rather than in an up and coming church?"

Answering the question, he said: "It means going to the very heart of the church's and the ministry's mission—'Pending through our purpose, our reason for being.'

"Dry rot," said the Rev. Oliver, "has currently set in on the church, particularly on the race question.

"Unless the church comes alive to the real issues of the world in which we live, it will not long be with us," he said. "We have too long pontificated or been preachy with our pious pronouncements."

Carrying it further, the young preacher said, "Maybe what the church needs is to become extreme in the gospel—to be an extremist."

And then he read a lengthy quotation from the Negro leader, Martin Luther King, "one who most of you would consider an extremist."

Quoting Dr. King's words, the Rev. Oliver said that Jesus Christ, Martin Luther, John Bunyan, Abraham Lincoln, the Apostle Paul and Thomas Jefferson were all "extremists."

"'Jesus Christ was an extremist for love, truth, and goodness and thereby rose above His environment,'" he continued to quote the Negro leader. "'So, after all, maybe the South, the nation and the world are in dire need of creative extremists.'"

He concluded the sermon by expressing a series of candid hopes for his old Dallas congregation located at Mockingbird Lane and

See PASTOR on Page

"The time has come for action. We must continue the essential ministry of Christ or get out of the business. I am dead sure about this. This means that church must be willing to give its own life to save it."

★ PASTOR

Continued From Page 25

Alderson in Northeast Dallas and the Church as a whole.

"New forms of urban life have revolutionized our world. The problems of housing and employment need the guidance and concern of the church. We have a new generation of those in need.

"I hope the church takes its place with those who are struggling all over the world for human rights, freedom and justice.

"We in the church are called to get our hands dirty by living in the midst of the world and not just standing on the sidelines making pious pronouncements."

JIM LEHRER ARTICLE ON BILL OLLIVER'S DECISION TO BECOME PASTOR OF BEAUMONT CHURCH.

Bill Oliver and
Laddie Melton

Al Price

SCLC Volunteers in Beaumont

BILL OLIVER'S INSTALLATION IN BEAUMONT

Plymouth Congregational
Church--Beaumont, TX

John Gibson—First
Director of POWER

Loretta Williams Oliver

March to support release of Wilmington 10. Bill Oliver in the center behind Ben Chavis' young daughter.

BILL OLIVER AND REP. CHARLIE RANGLE TESTIFYING
BEFORE CONGRESSIONL COMMITTEE.

RENEE OLIVER

AFRICAN MEETING HOUSE—
NANTUCKET, MA

Seven

FIELD REPRESENTATIVE FOR THE US COMMISSION ON CIVIL RIGHTS

A riot in Houston involving an estimated five hundred police and at least four hundred students at Texas Southern University (TSU) and a surreptitious meeting over the disappearance of an Oklahoma high school student were only two of the incidents that Bill Oliver became involved with in 1967 and 1968.

In early 1967, while still pastor of the Beaumont church, Bill accepted a position with the US Commission on Civil Rights. His reputation as a visible regional leader of the civil rights movement had moved well beyond Beaumont. He was asked to serve as the Field Representative for this federal commission in the states of Louisiana, Oklahoma, and Texas. The commission was created by Congress in 1957, and their website states, "Established as an independent, bipartisan, fact-finding federal agency, our mission is to inform the development of national civil rights policy and enhance enforcement of federal civil rights laws."

Bill held this paid position for two years, and it required that he travel within those states, responding to and investigating civil rights complaints. He worked with the State Advisory Committees in those states. Bill said, "The committees gave powerless people a vehicle to air their grievances." When a complaint was made to a state committee, it was Bill's job to investigate the legitimacy of the complaint, gather information, interview people, and report back to the state committee. If the complaint had significant merit, then the committee would hold a public hearing where the press was present.

On several occasions during our interviews, Bill said, "The press provided some protection from violence. However, the Justice Department at times worked to hold down the media reporting of racial incidents."

One of the major incidents occurred in May of 1967 at Texas Southern University in Houston, an all-black school in the heart of the city. Similar to the environment on many college campuses at the time, there had been civil rights demonstrations at TSU, and tensions had heighted within the police department. The HoustonPress.com

Field Representative for The US Commission on Civil Rights

website states that the chief of police was disliked within the black community because of "his strong-arm tactics. So when a rumor spread across the TSU campus that a black six-year-old had been shot by a white police officer earlier that day, the reaction was swift and angry. (In fact, it was a six-year-old white boy who had been wounded by another white boy.)"

The HoustonPress.com article, written in 2009, goes on to say, "Angry students gathered, more police arrived. Rocks and bottles were thrown. A shot rang out, wounding an officer in the thigh, and within minutes, a full-blown riot erupted. Over the next hours, HPD [the Houston Police] shot 3,000 rounds of shotgun and carbine into the building, and received return fire. Five hundred officers eventually stormed Lanier Hall."

A police officer was shot and killed during the melee, and more than 480 students were arrested that night but were then released the next morning. Five students were subsequently charged with the death of the officer, and eventually brought to trial, "but the charges were dismissed when the jury couldn't reach a verdict."

Bill was in Allendale, South Carolina, at the time of this incident, attending a US Commission on Civil Rights meeting concerning school desegregation. He immediately left the meeting and flew to Houston, where he spent three weeks investigating the incident for the commission. Recalling the interviews he conducted, he adds more detail on the event. "Dogs were let loose in the dorm, and several students were bitten. There were multiple bullet holes in the side of the dorm. One of the five students charged with the murder of the policeman was not even in Houston that night. Each of the five students had the reputation of being student activists in previous civil rights incidents at the university, and that's why they were arrested and tried. There is a belief that the police officer was killed by a shot from another officer."

The US Senate eventually appointed a committee to investigate the riot, and subsequently held a hearing. Along the way, it was discovered that the Department of Justice had helped fund a PhD dissertation by a doctoral student from Rice University, Blair Justice, that expounded a theory that a person could predict where and when a racial riot might occur based upon certain behavioral criteria. The dissertation examined other cities where such behavior had eventually led to riots. The Los Angeles racial riot was one such incident used to validate the theory. Bill says that the Houston police had used this study as a rationale that the environment at Texas Southern University was conducive to a riot and had prepared for a massive response to the initial incident with some five hundred police officers. The Senate hearings eventually concluded with no findings.

Bill states that one of the scariest incidents he had to investigate was in Idabel, Oklahoma, an area of the state

Field Representative for The US Commission on Civil Rights

referred to by some as Little Dixie. A young black girl who had planned to attempt to integrate the local high school suddenly disappeared, along with her family. Bill traveled to Oklahoma to interview the president of the local NAACP chapter. The environment was so volatile that the NAACP official refused to meet Bill in a public place but instead arranged to meet at a rural intersection outside of the city. "He was clearly frightened." When I asked Bill if he was afraid of holding this meeting, he said, "The NAACP official had enough fear for both of us."

The local sheriff claimed that the family had moved to Houston. Bill relates there was evidence of an unfinished meal on the kitchen table in the family's house. In addition, Bill was unsuccessful in getting the local superintendent of schools to meet with him. The state committee of the Civil Rights Commission held a hearing, but nothing ever resulted from it, and the family was never located.

The complaints that flowed to the state advisory committee did not always involve discrimination of African Americans. One incident involved the mistreatment by employers of Mexican farm workers in Rio Grande City. This was the first incident where Bill became involved in discrimination against Mexican farm workers. The workers organized a grape boycott supported by Caesar Chavez, who had organized several California boycotts by migrant workers. These boycotts generated widespread support and sympathy. In one incident, a group of nuns who were supporting the boycott were taken by police and held close to a moving freight train to frighten them. Bill's reports on the boycott resulted in congressional hearings being held in Texas by the Senate Agricultural Committee, and Senator Edward Kennedy attended the hearing.

The regional headquarters for the Civil Rights Commission was in Memphis, Tennessee; however, Bill was allowed to work out of his home in Beaumont. The Plymouth Church in Beaumont supported him in this federal position, although it sometimes took him away from his congregation. But his parishioners understood the importance of his broader civil rights activities.

After two years in the position, he was asked to take a new position and move to either Memphis or Washington, DC. The new position was financially attractive, a civil service grade GS-13, but he declined and resigned his position, remaining as pastor of the Beaumont church and continuing his activist role opposing social injustice of any kind in East Texas.

Eight

POWER

In the late 1960s, Bill's church needed help organizing and managing several projects and activities that the church saw as essential in the Beaumont community. Many community services and programs available for whites were either nonexistent for blacks, or their segregated facilities were insufficient or of poor quality. Thirty percent of the Beaumont population was black, and 25 percent of the city's housing was dilapidated. The Plymouth UCC church made application to the federal VISTA (Volunteers In Service To America) program to fund the hiring of workers to begin addressing those needs.

The application was approved, and twenty-five VISTA volunteers with a variety of skills moved to Beaumont to tackle the projects. They were housed in the education facility of the church, and even though the building was not designed as living quarters, it was an economical way to make the program a reality. They immediately began work on a day-care center to meet the needs of the black community. Most black families needed both parents to work in order to survive financially, and the care of their children was always a critical need.

After only one year, just as the workers had successfully begun to address the needs of the community, a county judge ruled that the program did not meet the federal VISTA requirements and convinced the governor to stop the funding. It was logical to expect that without this federal funding, the volunteers would pack up and leave; however, they recognized how important their work was, and twenty-three of them demonstrated their commitment to the program and stayed. This decision obviously resulted in a need for some other source of funding. After much agonizing and creative thinking, Bill and his associates were successful in getting a gift of $26,000 from a Republican foundation in Dallas, along with a gift of $10,000 from the United Church of Christ Division of Homeland Ministries.

They organized under the acronym POWER (People Organized With Economic Resources), and one of their critical responsibilities was the continual fundraising efforts to make certain the programs continued.

Power

Over the next several years, POWER's importance and influence grew in the community. The first executive director was John Gibson, who had worked for the Southern Christian Leadership Conference. He was followed by Ernesto Cortez, who had been involved in organizing the boycott of grape farmers. Cortez later headed up a neighborhood-community organization in Chicago. A third executive director was Gus Lyons, who is still in contact with Bill and who has established several other community organizations in Texas.

One of the ambitious and significant projects that the POWER workers became involved in was the Plymouth Village housing endeavor. This was a federally financed Housing for Urban Development (HUD) project to meet the housing needs of lower-income residents, regardless of race, color, or creed. In 1969, after a lengthy process, the Plymouth Village proposal received HUD approval, and construction commenced on ten acres of land owned by the Plymouth Church. The construction of nineteen buildings and 150 air-conditioned units was completed and dedicated in 1972. An important facility within the complex was the Plymouth Day Care Center, fulfilling day-care needs for lower-income families while parents were working.

Plymouth Village, a nonprofit organization, was managed by a board of directors made up principally of Plymouth Church members. Bill Oliver was closely involved in the original concept, the construction, and the ongoing management of the facility. It was during this project that Bill honed his computer skills. His first appreciation of the power of the computer occurred when he was organizing his door-to-door campaign for John F. Kennedy in 1960. When he arrived in Beaumont, he quickly realized the value of the computer in organizing voter-registration activities in the Beaumont and Port Arthur areas.

With the development of Plymouth Village, Bill built a computer-accounting system to handle the financial transactions of the facility. He purchased his first computer, an affordable Radio Shack model, and his expertise with information technology continued to grow to meet the needs of the community he was serving. Those computer skills and knowledge, born of necessity in Beaumont, would serve him well later in his career, in Hartford, Connecticut, and Nantucket, Massachusetts.

Plymouth Village still continues strong today, serving the white, Hispanic, and black communities in Beaumont.

Nine

UCC COMMISSION FOR SOCIAL JUSTICE

Many people in the community of Nantucket, where Bill Oliver now resides, are aware of his personal involvement in numerous racial justice activities in the 1960s and 1970s. However, Bill's definition of civil rights goes well beyond the disenfranchisement of blacks. He says that civil rights and justice must include the rights of people who have faced discrimination because of race, sexual orientation, nationality, women's rights, employment, poverty, and conscientious objection. His commitment throughout his adult life is a testimony to this. Bill emphasizes that all of these issues share the common challenge of "how do you disturb the silent majority on issues of social justice?"

He was actively involved in addressing employment discrimination of Mexican farm workers in Texas. He lobbied for a pro-choice organization on behalf of women's right to choose in Roe v. Wade. Although he would say that "I've never considered myself a pacifist," he willingly gave advice to young men who had been drafted during the Vietnam War and were opposed to that war. He specifically assisted them in filling out conscientious objector forms. When Dr. Martin Luther King Jr. voiced his objection to our involvement in that war, it quickly became an issue in the black community. Shortly after his move to New Haven in the mid-1980s, Bill took part in demonstrations opposing Yale University's investments in apartheid South Africa. And later, in the mid-1990s, he organized a sit-in and demonstration protesting Yale University's employment practices for its service workers.

The United Church of Christ was more sensitive to racial issues than most Protestant churches, and in the 1800s, its forerunner denomination, the Congregational Church, had established a large number of black churches, especially in the South. For example, the state of North Carolina had more than two hundred UCC black churches in the 1960s, most tracing their history back to the Civil War and before. Early in the 1960s, there

UCC Commission for Social Justice

was a demonstration at the UCC's Annual General Synod meeting in Boston, demanding the church take a more active and visible position on racial justice. As a result of this gathering, a committee called Ministers for Racial Justice was established. The name was soon changed to the Commission for Racial Justice Now, the name itself clearly stating its commitment.

When asked, "What motivated you to become an activist?" Bill quickly replied, "My sense of justice." Clearly showing his pastoral commitment, he added, "You're a pastor to your flock." Bill became a regional representative for the UCC commission in the late 1960s, and then became a member of the commission itself in 1971. He states that his work on the commission for more than a decade gave him "the most personal satisfaction" of any of his activities. He ultimately served as chairman of the commission for six years in the 1970s.

The commission had fifteen members around the country and had specific quotas of black membership, not only on the commission itself, but also on its boards and committees. Because of Bill's active involvement with the commission, he was able to influence the choice of those members from black churches, and as a result, several members of his Beaumont church served in various positions. Many other Protestant denominations formed boards or committees to address the racial discrimination issue, but the UCC commission was unique because of its strong representation from black churches within its denomination.

The ultimate name of the commisssion, the UCC Commission for Racial and Social Justice, operated in an advisory capacity for the denomination as a whole. It made itself available to local churches for education on social justice issues when they needed guidance on a particular subject, and provided advice on how to address specific racial problems that surfaced in local communities. On occasion, the commission took formal positions on issues and worked to influence the General Synod to adopt the position.

During his term as chairman of the commission, Bill became actively involved in opposing the North Carolina court decision known as the Wilmington Ten. This case, in which ten blacks were convicted in 1972 of conspiracy and arson, gained national and international attention as an example of racial injustice in the United States.

An all-black high school had been closed in Wilmington, and the students were distributed to white schools throughout the city in an attempt to integrate the school system. There was little warning given before the black school was closed, and the principal and most of the teachers at the school were terminated. Subsequently, there were several serious incidents of conflict between white and black students that eventually led to the blacks boycotting one school. These confrontations culminated in the firebombing of a local store. Several students and adults were arrested, and ten of them were eventually charged with the firebombing.

Among those arrested was Ben Chavis, a twenty-four-year-old seminary student, who was the Southern Region program director of the UCC Commission for Racial and Social Justice. The other nine individuals arrested were all high school students. Mr. Chavis had been sent to Wilmington by the UCC to try to calm the situation. Since he was the oldest of the group arrested, he was depicted as the leader and ultimately received the harshest prison sentence of thirty-four years.

The court decision quickly gained attention from groups across the country and around the world as one of obvious racial injustice. There were numerous demonstrations in support of the Wilmington Ten. Bill Oliver describes one such demonstration, where marchers from around the nation, including activist Angela Davis, came to Raleigh and marched around the state capitol building. Bill says the environment was "ominous," with signs in the windows of buildings and the white crowd yelling, "Kill the Wilmington Ten." He says he had real fear as he marched with the group since, "I was the only white face in the group of some two hundred."

Ben Chavis and the other nine students spent the next four years in prison. As extreme public pressure in opposition to the North Carolina judicial decision grew, the group was finally released on bond. The UCC, through its Commission for Racial and Social Justice, put up two hundred fifty thousand dollars for Ben Chavis's release.

In December 1980, the Federal District Court ordered a new trial and overturned the decision. Bill Oliver, as chairman of the UCC commission, played an active role in influencing the UCC to put forward the bond money. There was considerable objection within the UCC leadership to making the funds available; however, the persistence of the commission under Bill's leadership won the argument. Perhaps ironically, after the federal court overturned the decision, the bond money was returned to the UCC with interest, proving to be a good and sound investment from several angles.

There never was a new trial, but finally, in 2012, the governor of North Carolina pardoned the Wilmington Ten. Ben Chavis completed his education, a bachelor of science degree in chemistry from the University of North Carolina, a master of divinity from Duke, and a PhD from Howard University Theological Seminary. In 1985, he became executive director of the UCC Commission for Racial and Social Justice, and then executive director of the NAACP in 1993. A few years later, in 1980, he was a featured speaker at Bill Oliver's recognition dinner.

During his tenure on the UCC commission, Bill developed a friendship with Jeremiah (Jerry) Wright, pastor of the Trinity Church in Chicago, the church that Barack Obama attended before he became president. Jerry and Bill served together on various committees in the 1970s, long before Jerry's public comments caused candidate Obama to cut his ties with both Wright and the church. Bill was somewhat surprised at the furor surrounding the incident. He was very familiar with many all-black church services and their proclivity to embellish situations in order to emphasize a point. Their services are clearly much more emotional than traditional white services, and that fact alone leave many Caucasians uncomfortable. Add this to the heated environment of a presidential campaign, and the situation took on a life of its own. Over several years as the pastor of Trinity Church, Jerry Wright had grown the membership to more than three thousand members, the largest congregation in the United Church of Christ denomination.

Ten

Systemic Change

Bill Oliver's involvement in various activities in support of racial and social justice of all kinds did not follow a carefully planned agenda but rather was in response to the needs of those marginalized in our society. He has said, "I was the luckiest man alive to be at the right place at the right time. I had more fun than a barrel of monkeys."

Change not only was essential in the white community but also equally challenging within the black community. The attitude of many older blacks reminded him of the father in the film *The Butler*, who was fearful for his son's safety when he became a freedom rider. Bill wrestled with how to effect change in an environment of go along and get along that was inbred in the black community for generations, and a fundamental foundation of the Jim Crow culture. He emphasizes, "We had to work toward systemic change, rather than just providing separate services."

Historically, the Plymouth Church in Beaumont provided a variety of community services for blacks that were otherwise not available in the community. Separate playgrounds, day-care services, YMCA, a hospital, schools, and of course the churches themselves, were separate. Many blacks were satisfied with the separate but equal philosophy expounded by southern white leaders, even recognizing the inequality of the separation. But it was the safe route for blacks to go along. Bill took the position, "Are we for real change, or just to solve a service issue?"

Throughout his ministry, Bill consciously pushed the community toward systemic change. Demonstrations, boycotts, sit-ins, and even welcoming arrest were necessary actions to awaken the conscience of both the white and black communities to injustice. The visible involvement of youth in these demonstrations, not only college students, but also middle and high school students, was criticized by many, but essential for waking up the community. This tactic underscores the belief of many that change almost always comes from the idealism of youth.

One area of resistance came from the other black churches in the city. As Bill took the leadership role in this systemic change, he was considered by many of the clergy as a pariah. He said, "I got in their face." He tried to shame them into supporting the various efforts to effect social justice for the marginalized in the community. Bill's contrarian nature to challenge the status quo on social issues was an important quality in effecting systemic change.

Still another source of resistance was from the black school administration. One principal, strongly opposed to the sit-ins and demonstrations, threatened to suspend any students who participated. It took the personal involvement of Bill and other leaders to deter him from this action. Laddie Melton, Andrew's great uncle and a leader in the church and black community, told the principal, "Don't go picking on the kids who are demonstrating."

Throughout that time, Bill received criticism and resistance from other sources. One incident involved his grandfather, who was still the pastor of a Disciples of Christ church in northeast Texas. He was a well-respected minister within his denomination and had received an honorary doctor of law degree from Texas Christian University. On one occasion, Bill went to visit and preach at his grandfather's church and brought a black fellow parishioner with him. They stayed in the church parsonage with his grandfather. Subsequently,

Systemic Change

his grandfather was strongly criticized for "having a preacher from a black church preach in their church and for having a black stay in the parsonage." Bill's grandfather resigned from the pastorate over the incident and retired from the ministry. Bill says, "It was a moment of activism for my grandfather."

During his pastorate in Beaumont, both his father and his grandfather preached at the Plymouth Church on numerous occasions.

Eleven

Political Activities

"A lot of my work was openly political, but not as a candidate for office. I believe that my role was to impact policy and open doors for others, especially the marginalized in our society." From the moment Bill Oliver arrived in Beaumont and truly began to understand the magnitude of social injustice, especially as seen and experienced by his African American parishioners, he saw that a major part of the solution lay within the political process.

The laws and regulations that supported segregation, and the fact that blacks were not represented among the local, county, and state elected officials, had created and supported the continuation of black disenfranchisement.

Political Activities

Underpinning this political system in the South were specific legal and regulatory barriers, not to mention physical and emotional threats and intimidation to keep blacks from registering to vote and away from the polls.

From Bill's first sign of political activism in 1960 as a volunteer worker during the Kennedy presidential campaign, and his speech at the Austin, Texas, rally in 1963 that coincided with Dr. King's March on Washington, DC., Bill's political activities grew exponentially. Over the next twenty years in Beaumont, he organized voter registration, lobbied for elimination of the poll tax, worked to eliminate gerrymandered districts, went to court to define representative districts, and managed more than ten local, county, state, and federal campaigns for political office. He said, "If you're going to make change, you've got to have political power. I was lucky enough to be part of a host of events, local, statewide, and national, which played a significant part in changing America, like the Selma to Montgomery march that led to the 1965 Voting Rights Law."

As mentioned earlier in this biography, Bill worked with his parishioners to "sell" poll taxes, the process of helping people within the black community fill out voter-registration documents, and in many cases finding the money to pay for the poll tax so they could vote. It was not until 1972 that the poll tax in Texas was declared unconstitutional. However, intimidation to discourage blacks from voting continued. Voter registration focused on getting control of local and district elections so the disenfranchised black voters could elect officials who were sympathetic to their needs.

Also, as mentioned previously, the Democratic Party was allowed under state law to hold all-white primaries. In addition, people were prevented from voting on the school budget unless they were property owners. In the state of Texas, county commissioners were directly elected in separate statewide elections and held great influence and power. Under state law, they controlled the rivers, roads, and railroads.

In addition to the task of registering voters, the gerrymandered voting districts needed to be drastically changed before there would be a chance of electing an African American and correcting the problem of the diminution of black voters. Bill turned to the computer to identify how to restructure the voting districts to more accurately and fairly represent the disenfranchised citizens. Over several years, he became an expert in this area, and directed activities to redistrict the Beaumont and Port Arthur areas. These efforts frequently required going to court to demonstrate that the old districts were not truly representative. Dave Richards, a lawyer in Houston and husband of future governor Ann Richards, was a critical resource

Political Activities

in representing Bill's redistricting efforts before the Texas courts.

It was not until 1972 that the voting districts in southeastern Texas, following several legal battles, truly became more representative. Bill had convinced his friend Al Price to run for the Texas legislature, but he was defeated three times before finally being elected in 1972. Bill proudly states, "I had drawn Al Price's legislative district." Once elected to office, Representative Price served for the next twenty years, and Bill ran his campaigns until he moved to Connecticut in the 1980s.

In addition, Bill was campaign manager for Mickey Leland, who represented the Eighteenth US Congressional District in the Houston area. Congressman Leland, an African American pharmacist from Houston, served three terms in the US Congress, and Bill also ran his reelection campaigns.

As a result of his successful redistricting efforts, Bill was considered an expert on redistricting matters. He was subsequently called upon to testify before a US congressional committee on voting rights, especially concerning the fairness and accuracy of redistricting issues. He emphasizes, "I had the census data to back up redistricting."

During the mid-1960s, Bill had become disillusioned with the Texas Democratic Party and became active in the Liberal Party, a party he felt better recognized the needs of the disenfranchised voter. He served as chairman of the Texas Liberal Party in 1966. However, by 1968, he had returned to the Democratic Party, and he and Loretta attended the National Democratic Convention in Chicago that year. He later attended the Democratic Conventions in 1972 and 1984.

Twelve

RECOGNITION DINNER

The average length of a minister's pastorate in Protestant churches is around six years, a short period of time for most professions, but some church hierarchies follow a practice of moving their ministers after even a shorter period of time. In other Protestant churches where the local membership retains the authority to hire and fire pastors, the length of service may be somewhat longer. The fact is that after a few years, a congregation consciously or subconsciously frequently feels that the pastor has given all he or she can to their church, and that it is time for new ideas and a new direction.

However, Bill Oliver broke this pattern in a significant way, serving the Beaumont church for twenty-three years. Even without the specific successes of his leadership in numerous social justice activities that have been detailed in the foregoing pages, the length of his pastorate itself speaks volumes about how successful he was and the respect his parishioners had for him.

In 1980, after almost seventeen years in Beaumont, Bill's congregation and the community organized an evening of recognition for his service. The attendees at the dinner were a reflection of Bill's civil rights, political, and other social justice activities during those years. The April 27, 1980, edition of the *Beaumont Sunday Enterprise*, in an extensive article covering the event said, "And at 6:00 p.m. Wednesday, at the civic center, noted state Democrats like Bob Krueger, Mickey Leland and Jack Brooks will join fellow United Church of Christ clergymen, like former Ambassador Andrew Young and Wilmington Ten defendant Ben Chavis, in honoring Oliver in the midst of his 16th year as pastor of the active Beaumont congregation." In addition, Rev. Reuben Shears, a UCC official who in Bill's early years had defended him in the attempt to rein him in and replace him in Beaumont, was present.

The newspaper went on to quote Al Price, who said, "One of the reasons for the list of dignitaries coming to this affair is Bill Oliver has been very active in electing people responsive to the little people." Congressman

Recognition Dinner

Brooks, who had not always been supportive of Bill's civil rights activities, canceled his own campaign fundraising dinner, attended Bill's dinner, and helped finance the event. Even a conservative district federal judge who had made several rulings over the years in opposition to civil rights came to the dinner.

Bill's wife, Loretta, was quoted in the same article, "Bill's extroverted, aggressive. He has a lot of energy. He'll work all night. Occasionally he'll die on me. He's basically a romantic. But he and I believe the way you change certain things is through political action. He'd miss being in the pulpit. He'd almost talk to any listener he can find. A church is people, not a building. If you gave Bill a nine-to-five job, he'd go bananas."

Throughout Bill's career, there were several somewhat humorous moments among his various social justice activities. The birth of his and Loretta's first child, an almost unheard of product of a mixed marriage in the South, caused some to question whether the child would be born striped or with polka dots. On one occasion, Loretta and Bill's mother were in a department store and as they approached an escalator, Bill's mother went to hand the new light-skinned infant to Loretta. A white woman stepped in and asked, "Wouldn't you prefer to let me take the baby for you?"

On another occasion, an FBI official visited Bill's home to inquire about leaflets he had printed in opposition to the Vietnam War. While the official was there, Bill received a call and had to leave for several minutes, and he asked the official if he would look after the baby. When Bill returned, he found the official had changed young Bill's diaper. In later years, the official would say that was the only time in his career that he had to change a diaper when he was on official FBI business.

On still another occasion involving young Bill, he and his father were engaged in a protest in Austin, Texas, and Bill had a photo of his three-year-old son carrying a poster that said, "Freedom Now."

The actress Shirley MacLaine was at one time planning a visit to Red China with a group of women representing all facets of American life. Surprisingly, Bill was contacted and asked if he could provide the name of a female Ku Klux Klan member. He contacted a KKK acquaintance and was given a name. Shirley MacLaine subsequently came to Beaumont, visited with Bill, and interviewed the woman, who ultimately made the trip to China.

Loretta's parents had rarely traveled far from Beaumont, but Bill and Loretta took them to a United Church of Christ Annual Synod meeting in Philadelphia. On their return, they stopped in Washington, DC, and went to make a call on their congressman. As they were going through the metal security detector, an alarm went off. Unbeknown to Bill, his mother-in-law routinely carried a small loaded pistol in her handbag. After some delay

Recognition Dinner

and anxious moments, they were allowed into the building; however, the guard held the pistol for safekeeping.

Al Price, Bill's close friend and representative to the Texas legislature from the Beaumont district, was also a member of the Central Committee of the World Council of Churches. On an official visit to East Germany prior to the tearing down of the Berlin Wall, Al visited a church and went to read a religious tract on a wall. To his surprise, the picture on the cover was of Bill and Al at a civil rights protest in Texas.

As Bill relates these light-hearted incidents, he emphasizes that they are an important part of his story, and in their own way, these stories give some background about the racial environment in East Texas during his years in Beaumont.

Bill's pastorate in Beaumont would continue for another six years, a total of twenty-three years, before he moved to New Haven, Connecticut. He and his wife, Loretta, had divorced a few years prior to the move. His oldest son, Bill Oliver IV, later settled in the New Haven area after graduation from college and inherited his father's computer interest and skills. He is an information technology professional working with municipalities. Bill's second son, David, is also employed in the information technology field, in Austin, Texas.

Thirteen

THE MOVE TO NEW HAVEN

*E*arlier, this memoir mentioned two of the individuals Bill Oliver said were most influential in his life. The first, and perhaps the most significant, was Rev. Dr. W. B. J. Martin, his mentor at the Perkins School of Theology and the pastor of the First Community Congregational Church in Dallas. The second person was Al Price, the close personal friend in Beaumont who was, after three attempts, finally elected to the Texas legislature, a result of Bill's successful efforts to reconfigure the voting district and eliminate gerrymandering that had previously guaranteed a Caucasian candidate would be elected.

The third person Bill mentioned as being very influential in his life was Rev. Dr. Edwin Edmunds, the

The Move to New Haven

pastor of the Dixwell Avenue Congregational Church in Hartford, Connecticut. Bill first became acquainted with Dr. Edmunds when they both were active on the United Church of Christ (UCC) Commission for Racial Justice. Before moving to Hartford, Dr. Edmunds had been president of the NAACP chapter in Greensboro, North Carolina, where he was pastor of a local church. He was legally blind and a light-skinned African American who could pass for white.

In 1986, after serving as pastor of the Beaumont Plymouth Church for twenty-three years, Bill felt it was time for a change. In his narrative résumé, Bill states, "That move was triggered by the opportunity to become associate minister of the Dixwell Avenue Congregational Church—UCC. This is the oldest African American Congregational church in America, and has had a unique history reflecting its heritage and outstanding leadership. The condition of my call included an opportunity to proctor for Dr. Edwin Edmunds the Black and White in America course at Southern Connecticut University (for fourteen years). Such a teaching experience expanded and kept current my knowledge of African American history in this country."

The Dixwell church did not have enough funds to hire a full-time associate minister, so Bill called upon the computer skills he had developed over the previous two decades in Beaumont and became employed full-time as director of technology for the New Haven public schools. His personal narrative states, "I designed and guided the installation of computer systems for the forty-seven schools, including the city-wide network, all managed by my office in the administration building. The annual budget for computer projects often exceeded ten million dollars."

Not long after he arrived in New Haven, Bill again took up the banner for social justice. He refused to attend the local Rotary Club because it had no black or women members. He also played an active role in changing the investment policies of Yale University. Yale, along with many other American institutions, had some of its endowment funds invested in apartheid South Africa. Demonstrations ensued to force the university to divest itself of those investments and in doing so hopefully put pressure on South Africa to cease the racial injustice of its segregation policies.

Also, he again became involved in managing a political campaign. That campaign was successful in electing the first black mayor of New Haven.

In the mid-1990s, he took on Yale University again. The clerical and maintenance workers, members of the Federation of University Employees Union, were embroiled in a contract dispute with the university. The Rev. Jessie Jackson, chairman of the Rainbow Coalition, came to the city on graduation day in 1996

The Move to New Haven

to show support for the unions. Bill had helped organize a demonstration to take place at the same time as the university graduation ceremonies. Many of the graduates carried placards and wore buttons that said, "Yale Settle." Three to five thousand people engaged in the peaceful demonstration, and subsequently, more than three hundred were arrested for a sit-in in front of the administration building. The university eventually settled with the union.

After moving to Nantucket in 2000, Bill was invited back to the Dixwell church in October 2013 to preach the installation sermon for Rev. Gerry Streets. Ironically, Rev. Streets had previously been the chaplain at Yale.

Fourteen

THE MOVE TO NANTUCKET

In 2000, Bill and his third wife, Renee, whom he had married in Austin, Texas, in 1990, moved to Nantucket Island, a small island some twenty-six miles at sea off the coast of Cape Cod in Massachusetts. Renee had family connections to the island, and she and Bill had vacationed there on occasion.

Bill, in a printed résumé, states, "I retired and moved to Nantucket, Massachusetts. In the fall of 2000, I took the job of director of technology for the Nantucket public schools. Between 2000 and my new retirement (2006) from Nantucket schools, I built a computer network for all the school buildings, linking the town and the schools. Under my leadership, our schools became one of the top

The Move to Nantucket

3 percent of schools in Massachusetts as regards to the ratio of computers to students. After retiring from the Nantucket schools, I continued as a consultant for an additional one and a half years, until they were able to find a replacement for me."

Probably because of the predominance of Quakers in the commercial and spiritual life of Nantucket throughout most of the eighteetnth century, the island has a history of being proactive on social issues during the nineteenth century.

As an island dependent on the whaling industry, much of its male population was away on voyages for two and three years at a time, so of necessity, Nantucket women in many instances ran the island. The fact that Quakers believed that young girls and boys should receive the same education prepared young women for such activity. This undoubtedly led to the island's visible and early support for women's rights.

It also had a significant black population, many of whom were employed in the whaling industry, and had developed more sensitivity to discrimination issues than was true on the mainland. In 1846, almost fifteen years before the Civil War, the Nantucket schools provided equal education for blacks. In the mid-1840s, Frederick Douglass, who later became a national leader in the abolitionist movement, was invited to speak at a public gathering on the island, one of his first public speeches against slavery.

Bill and Renee, who was a teacher in the Nantucket public schools, became interested and involved in preserving the African American history of the island. The African American meeting hall on the island was built in the 1820s and is on the National Register of Historic Places. Throughout its history, the hall has been used as a church, a meeting house, and a school. After years of neglect in the twentieth century, the building was purchased in 1989 by the Boston-based Museum of African American History. During the 1990s, the building was restored. The property also includes the birthplace home of Absalom Boston, the first African American captain of a whale ship. The house was built in the late 1700s and is currently being restored.

Shortly after Bill and his wife, Renee, moved to the island, they were selected as site managers for the museum, overseeing a variety of programs for both local islanders and tourists. During their tenure as managers, the museum became much more visible, and the frequency of programs offered to the community increased markedly. Renee died in June 2012 after a long struggle with cancer, and Bill retired from his position at the museum in 2013.

At an event at the African Meeting House on Nantucket to honor Bill Oliver on his retirement, Beverly Morgan-Welsh, the executive director of the Museum of African American History, concisely summed up Bill as a "good man, a good and faithful servant." Throughout his

The Move to Nantucket

life, Bill's commitment to social justice, to those disenfranchised in our society, clearly underscores his chosen profession as a pastor to the people.

After moving to Nantucket, in an interview with the *Nantucket Inquirer and Mirror,* Bill is quoted as saying, "Much of my life has been like that. I happened to be in the right place at the right time, or the wrong place at the wrong time—whatever. And I've had more fun than you could ever imagine. You couldn't sit down and schedule all the things I've had a chance to do. I'm still on two legs, and hopefully I've got some wisdom that came out of it."

Bill continues to have personal contact with many people whom he was involved with during his years as a civil rights activist. In any discussion with him about his experiences, his passion for the ongoing need for systemic change to eliminate social injustice of all kinds is clearly evident.

References

Following is a list of references and sources that were used in writing this memoir:

"50th Anniversary of the March on Washington," National Action Network, [Date of article or access, complete URL of this article.]

"African Meeting House," Museum of African American History. afroammuseum.org/bhtn_site9.htm.

Baker, Eliot, "Bill Oliver Remembers…," *The Inquirer and Mirror*, February. 2009

"Beaumont Pastor to be Honored," *Beaumont News*, March 19, 1980.

"Bill Oliver," Profiles 1980, *Beaumont Sunday Enterprise*, April 27, 1980

"Black History Trail on Nantucket," Museum of African American History, afroammuseum.org/bhtn_intro.htm

"1965 Selma to Montgomery March Fast Facts," http://cnn.com/2013/09/15/us/1965-selma-to-montgomery-fast-facts/index.html

"Florence Higginbotham House," Museum of African American History, afroammuseum.org/bhtn_site10.htm

Goodwyn, Larry,, "Hey-You in Huntsville," *The Texas Observer*, August 6, 1965

"History of Wiley College" page on Wiley College website, [URL].

"Houston 101: An Earlier Time When Shots Rang Out At TSU," *Houston Press*, 07/2009

"Invictus," *The Economist*, December 14, 2013, p 15

Johnson, Robert, "Black-White Relations on Nantucket," *Historic Nantucket*, Spring 2002 issue.

Kartunner, Frances Ruley, "The Portrait of Absalom Boston," *Historic Nantucket, Vol. 55, No. 1 (Winter 2006), p 11-14.*

The King Center website, www.thekingcenter.org.

King Jr., Martin Luther, "Letter From The Birmingham Jail," April 16, 1963.

Lehrer, Jim, "Come Alive, Church Told," *The Dallas Times Herald*, City News, September 2, 1963.

Moore, Sarah, "Al Price Remembered," *Beaumont Enterprise*, October 25, 2013.

"New Minister Profile: Rev. Dr. Frederick "Jerry" Streets, Dixwell Avenue United Church of Christ, *The Connecticut Conference United Church of Christ*, http//www.ctucc.org/news/20140122_jerrystreets.html.

References

Olson, James, "Beaumont Riot of 1943," Texas State Historical Association, www.tshaonline.org/handbook/online/articles/jcb01.

Richards, Parker, "Oliver Honored by African Meeting House," *The Inquirer and Mirror,* June 26, 2014

Texas Southern University: Born In Sin, A College Finally Makes Houston Listen, (Cambridge, MA: Harvard University Press, 5/22/1967

16th Street Baptist Church Bombing, Wikipedia page, http://en.wikipedia.org/wiki/16th_Street_Baptist_Church_bombing.

Abernathy, Ralph, Wikipedia page, http//en.wikipedia.org/wiki/Ralph_Abernathy

Beaumont, Texas, Wikipedia page, http://en.wikipedia.org/wiki/Beaumont,_Texas.

Brooks, Jack, Wikipedia page, http://en.wikipedia.org/wiki/Jack_Brooks_(politician).

Chavis, Benjamin, Wikipedia page, http://en.wikipedia.org/wiki/Benjamin_Chavis

Civil Rights Act of 1964, Wikipedia page, http://en.wikipedia.org/wiki/Civil_Rights_Act_of_1964.

Evers, Medgar, Wikipedia page, http://en.wikipedia.org/wiki/Medgar_Evers.

Frazier, E. Franklin, Wikipedia page, http://en.wikipedia.org/wiki/E._Franklin_Frazier.

Freedom Summer, Wikipedia page, http://en.wikipedia.org/wiki/Freedom_Summer.

The Great Debaters, Wikipedia page, http://en.wikipedia.org/wiki/The_Great_Debaters.

Huntsville, Texas, Wikipedia page, http://en.wikipedia.org/wiki/Huntsville,_Texas.

Invisible Man, Wikipedia page, http://en.wikipedia.org/wiki/Invisible_Man.

Leland, Mickey, Wikipedia page, http://en.wilipedia.org/wiki/Mickey_Leland

March Against Fear, Wikipedia page, http://en.wikipedia.org/wiki/March_Against_Fear.

Nash, Diane, Wikipedia page, http://en.wikipedia.org/wiki/Diane_Nash.

Schwerner, Michael, Wikipedia page, http://en.wikipedia.org/wiki/Michael_Schwerner

Selma to Montgomery March, Wikipedia page, http://en.wikipedia.org/wiki/Selma_to_Montgomery_marches.

Tulsa Race Riot, Wikipedia page, http://en.wikipedia.org/wiki/Tulsa_race_riot.

US Commission on Civil Rights, Wikipedia page, http://en.wikipedia.org/wiki/U_S_Commission_on_Civil_Rights.

Voting Rights Act of 1965, Wikipedia page, http://en.wikipedia.org/wiki/Voting_Rights_Act_of_1965.

References

Wikipedia—Encyclopedia—Marshall, Texas, Wikipedia page, http://en.wikipedia.org/wiki/Marshall,_Texas.

Wilmington Ten, Wikipedia page, http://en.wikipedia.org/wiki/Wilmington_Ten.

Winnie, Texas, Wikipedia page, http://en.wikipedia.org/wiki/Winnie,_Texas.

Young, Andrew, Wikipedia page, http://en.wikipedia.org/wiki/Andrew_Young.

"The Wilmington Ten," This Month in North Carolina History, [URL].

Made in the USA
Charleston, SC
25 March 2015